Keeping Government Secrets: A Pocket Guide on the State-Secrets Privilege, the Classified Information Procedures Act, and Classified Information Security Officers

Second Edition

Robert Timothy Reagan

Federal Judicial Center
2013

This Federal Judicial Center publication was undertaken in furtherance of the Center's statutory mission to develop and conduct research and education programs for the judicial branch. While the Center regards the content as responsible and valuable, it does not reflect policy or recommendations of the Board of the Federal Judicial Center.

second printing

Contents

Introduction

As courts adjudicate cases involving classified information, they must protect government secrets. The Classified Information Procedures Act (CIPA) provides procedures for protecting classified information in criminal prosecutions. Similar procedures are used in civil cases. The courts are assisted in their protection of government secrets by classified information security officers provided by a small office in the Department of Justice's Management Division called the Litigation Security Group.

I. Classified Information

Classified information is information designated by the executive branch as not subject to public discussion.

> Our democratic principles require that the American people be informed of the activities of their Government. Also, our Nation's progress depends on the free flow of information both within the Government and to the American people. Nevertheless, throughout our history, the national defense has required that certain information be maintained in confidence in order to protect our citizens, our democratic institutions, our homeland security, and our interactions with foreign nations.[1]

The Classified Information Procedures Act defines "classified information" as

> information or material that has been determined by the United States Government pursuant to an Executive order, statute, or regulation, to require protection against unauthorized disclosure for reasons of national security and any restricted data, as defined in paragraph r. of section 11 of the Atomic Energy Act of 1954 (42 U.S.C. 2014(y)).[2]

The Act, in turn, defines "national security" as "the national defense and foreign relations of the United States."[3] Information is classified by an "original classification authority," whose

---

1. Exec. Order No. 13,526, 75 Fed. Reg. 707 (2010).
2. Pub. L. No. 96-456, 94 Stat. 2025, *as amended*, 18 U.S.C. app. 3 § 1(a) (2011).
3. *Id.* § 1(b).

authority to classify information emanates from the President through delegation authority specified by executive order.[4]

There are three levels of classification: (1) confidential, (2) secret, and (3) top secret. Confidential information is "information, the unauthorized disclosure of which reasonably could be expected to cause damage to the national security that the original classification authority is able to identify or describe."[5] Secret information is "information, the unauthorized disclosure of which reasonably could be expected to cause *serious* damage to the national security that the original classification authority is able to identify or describe."[6] Top secret information is "information the unauthorized disclosure of which reasonably could be expected to cause *exceptionally grave* damage to the national security that the original classification authority is able to identify or describe."[7]

Generally, access to classified information requires a security clearance.[8] Article III judges are automatically entitled to access to classified information necessary to resolve issues before them, but magistrate judges and law clerks must obtain security clearances to have access to classified information.[9]

Government attorneys and private attorneys may be cleared to see classified information, and attorneys may have clearances to see classified information that their clients cannot see.[10]

---

4. Exec. Order No. 13,526 § 1.3, 75 Fed. Reg. 707 (2010); *see* Presidential Order, Dec. 29, 2009, 75 Fed. Reg. 735 (2010) (listing classification authorities for secret and top secret classifications).

5. Exec. Order No. 13,526 § 1.2(a)(3), 75 Fed. Reg. 707 (2010).

6. *Id.* § 1.2(a)(2) (emphasis added).

7. *Id.* § 1.2(a)(1) (emphasis added).

8. *E.g.*, United States v. Bin Laden, 58 F. Supp. 2d 113, 118 (S.D.N.Y. 1999).

9. Security Procedures Established Pursuant to PL 96-456, 94 Stat. 2025, by the Chief Justice of the United States for the Protection of Classified Information ¶ 4, effective Jan. 15, 2011, *superseding* 18 U.S.C. app. 3 § 9 note (2011) (originally issued Feb. 12, 1981), *reproduced as* Appendix B [hereinafter Courts' Security Procedures]; United States v. Smith, 899 F.2d 564 (6th Cir. 1990) (holding that executive branch investigations of court staff for security clearances do not violate the constitutional separation of powers); *see* Robert Timothy Reagan, National Security Case Management: An Annotated Guide 1, 7–8 (Federal Judicial Center 2011) (noting that clearance for magistrate judges is greatly facilitated by the background checks they undergo when they become judges).

10. *In re* Terrorist Bombings of U.S. Embassies in E. Africa, 552 F.3d 93, 103, 116–30 (2d Cir. 2008); United States v. Abu Ali, 528 F.3d 210, 253 (4th Cir. 2008);

Compartmentation can provide an additional layer of security. "Sensitive Compartmented Information is information that
not only is classified for national security reasons as Top Secret,
Secret, or Confidential, but also is subject to special access and
handling requirements because it involves or derives from par-
ticularly sensitive intelligence sources and methods."[11] Usually
sensitive compartmented information is top secret information,
access to which is restricted to a limited set of individuals on a
need-to-know basis specific to the information.[12]

Courts do not have authority to overrule classification determinations.[13]

II. The State-Secrets Privilege

The government has a common-law right to keep state secrets
secret.[14]

A. Contract Cases

If litigation of a contract term requires the disclosure of state
secrets, then the term may be nonjusticiable.

The Supreme Court determined in *Totten v. United States*
that the survivor of an alleged Civil War spy could not recover
from the government unpaid compensation for the spying.[15]

> It may be stated as a general principle, that public poli-
> cy forbids the maintenance of any suit in a court of justice,
> the trial of which would inevitably lead to the disclosure of
> matters which the law itself regards as confidential, and re-
> specting which it will not allow the confidence to be violated.
> On this principle, suits cannot be maintained which would re-
> quire a disclosure of the confidences of the confessional, or

see Robert Timothy Reagan, Confidential Discovery: A Pocket Guide on Protective Orders 15 (Federal Judicial Center 2012).

11. 28 C.F.R. § 17.18(a) (2011).

12. *See* Reagan, *supra* note 9, at 12.

13. United States v. Fernandez, 913 F.2d 148, 154 (4th Cir. 1990); United
States v. Musa, 833 F. Supp. 752, 755 (E.D. Mo. 1993).

14. Gen. Dynamics Corp. v. United States, 563 U.S. 478, ___, 131 S. Ct. 1900,
1906 (2011) (slip op. at 6–7) (contracts); United States v. Reynolds, 345 U.S. 1,
6–8 (1952) (torts).

15. 92 U.S. 105 (1876).

those between husband and wife, or of communications by a client to his counsel for professional advice, or of a patient to his physician for a similar purpose. Much greater reason exists for the application of the principle to cases of contract for secret services with the government, as the existence of a contract of that kind is itself a fact not to be disclosed.[16]

The Supreme Court applied *Totten* to a Cold War analog in *Tenet v. Doe.*[17] According to the complaint, the government failed to honor an agreement to provide support for life to a defecting high-ranking diplomat and his wife from a former enemy in exchange for their acting as spies for several years before completing their defection.[18]

In 2011, the Supreme Court determined that because litigation of a defense to a contract claim would require unacceptable disclosure of state secrets, the courts should leave the parties where they found them on that claim.[19] *General Dynamics Corp. v. United States* involved a multibillion-dollar contract to develop a stealth aircraft for the Navy, which ran into difficulties in designing a stealth craft that could land on an aircraft carrier.[20] The key dispute was whether the government had terminated the contract for default and was entitled to a refund of $1.35 billion or whether the government had terminated the contract for convenience and was required to reimburse the contractors $1.2 billion.[21] Litigation of the issue required the courts to determine whether the government had withheld from the contractors secret superior knowledge.[22] Because what the government knew was a state secret, the $2.55-billion dispute was nonjusticiable.[23]

> The contract itself was a classified document at one point. Both parties—the Government no less than petitioners—must have assumed the risk that state secrets would prevent the adjudication of claims of inadequate performance.

16. *Id.* at 107.
17. 544 U.S. 1 (2005).
18. *Id.* at 3–5.
19. Gen. Dynamics Corp. v. United States, 563 U.S. 478, 131 S. Ct. 1900 (2011).
20. *Id.* at ___, 131 S. Ct. at 1 (slip op. at 1–2).
21. *Id.* at ___, 131 S. Ct. at 1903–05, 1908–09 (slip op. at 2, 4–5, 10–11).
22. *Id.* at ___, 131 S. Ct. at 1904 (slip op. at 2–4).
23. *Id.* at ___, 131 S. Ct. at 1907, 1909 (slip op. at 7–9, 12).

... [C]ontracting parties ... can negotiate, for example, the timing and amount of progress payments to account for the possibility that state secrets may ultimately render the contract unenforceable.[24]

B. Tort Cases

In tort cases, the state-secrets privilege acts as an evidentiary privilege.

In the 1952 case, *United States v. Reynolds*, three civilian observers were among those killed when a B-29 bomber crashed on October 6, 1948, during a flight to test secret electronic equipment.[25] The observers' widows sued the government and sought to discover the Air Force's official accident investigation report and investigative statements of the three surviving crew members.[26] The Supreme Court determined that the evidence was subject to a privilege against revealing military secrets.[27]

The district court had ordered production and awarded the plaintiffs damages as a sanction for the government's failure to produce the evidence and refusal to allow ex parte in camera inspection by the court.[28] The Secretary of the Air Force filed a formal claim of privilege in response to the production order, and the Air Force's judge advocate general filed an affidavit declaring that production of the evidence would seriously hamper national security.[29] The government offered as a substitute production of the surviving crew members for examination as witnesses.[30] The Supreme Court, which did not examine the classified evidence, determined that the proposed substitute was adequate.[31]

> The privilege belongs to the Government and must be asserted by it; it can neither be claimed nor waived by a private party. It is not to be lightly invoked. There must be a formal claim of privilege, lodged by the head of the department which has

24. *Id.* at ___, 131 S. Ct. at 1909 (slip op. at 12).
25. 345 U.S. 1, 2–3 (1952).
26. *Id.* at 3.
27. *Id.* at 6; *see* Doe v. CIA, 576 F.3d 95, 101–06 (2d Cir. 2009) (analyzing *Reynolds*).
28. *Reynolds*, 345 U.S. at 4–5.
29. *Id.*
30. *Id.* at 5.
31. *Id.* at 11.

control over the matter, after actual personal consideration by that officer. The court itself must determine whether the circumstances are appropriate for the claim of privilege, and yet do so without forcing a disclosure of the very thing the privilege is designed to protect.[32]

The Supreme Court was not persuaded that the privileged evidence was necessary to the plaintiffs' case.[33] The government "formally offered to make the surviving crew members available for examination. We think that offer should have been accepted."[34]

In some cases, courts have dismissed tort actions on a finding that the cases could not be litigated because of privileged evidence.[35]

C. Invocation of the Privilege

There are three steps to invocation of the state-secrets privilege.[36] First, the privilege must be (1) invoked by the United States government[37] (2) by formal claim made by the head of the department controlling the secret[38] (3) after personal review of the matter.[39] Second, the court must determine that the secret information is legitimately secret, in which case it is absolutely

---

32. *Id.* at 7–8 (footnotes omitted).

33. *Id.* at 12.

34. *Id.*

35. *E.g.*, Mohamed v. Jeppesen Dataplan, Inc., 614 F.3d 1070 (9th Cir. 2010); El-Masri v. United States, 479 F.3d 296 (4th Cir. 2007).

36. *El-Masri*, 479 F.3d at 304.

37. *Id.*; Bareford v. Gen. Dynamics Corp., 973 F.2d 1138, 1141 (5th Cir. 1992); Zuckerbraun v. Gen. Dynamics Corp., 935 F.2d 544, 546 (2d Cir. 1991); Fitzgerald v. Penthouse Int'l Ltd., 776 F.2d 1236, 1239 n.4 (4th Cir. 1985); Ellsberg v. Mitchell, 709 F.2d 51, 56 (D.C. Cir. 1983).

38. *El-Masri*, 479 F.3d at 304; Sterling v. Tenet, 416 F.3d 338, 345 (4th Cir. 2005); McDonnell Douglas Corp. v. United States, 323 F.3d 1006, 1022 (Fed. Cir. 2003); Kasza v. Browner, 133 F.3d 1159, 1169 (9th Cir. 1998); *Bareford*, 973 F.2d at 1141; *Zuckerbraun*, 935 F.2d at 546; Halkin v. Helms, 690 F.2d 977, 991 (D.C. Cir. 1982); *Fitzgerald*, 776 F.2d at 1242; Halpern v. United States, 258 F.2d 36, 38 (2d Cir. 1958).

39. *El-Masri*, 479 F.3d at 304; *Sterling*, 416 F.3d at 345; *Kasza*, 133 F.3d at 1169; *Bareford*, 973 F.2d at 1141–42; *Zuckerbraun*, 935 F.2d at 546; *Halkin*, 690 F.2d at 991; *Halpern*, 258 F.2d at 38.

protected.[40] Third, the court must determine how protection of the secret affects the case.[41]

D. Secrecy Validity

The court does not determine what information should be secret, but it does have the responsibility to determine what information legitimately has the status of a state secret.

> Judicial control over the evidence in a case cannot be abdicated to the caprice of executive officers. Yet we will not go so far as to say that the court may automatically require a complete disclosure to the judge before the claim of privilege will be accepted in any case. It may be possible to satisfy the court, from all the circumstances of the case, that there is a reasonable danger that compulsion of the evidence will expose military matters which, in the interest of national security, should not be divulged. When this is the case, the occasion for the privilege is appropriate, and the court should not jeopardize the security which the privilege is meant to protect by insisting upon an examination of the evidence, even by the judge alone, in chambers.[42]

Courts sometimes review classified information to determine what information is properly designated as secret.[43] Judicial review of classified evidence or arguments may not be necessary if the public record sufficiently establishes the need to keep the evidence secret.[44] Whether or not the court reviews classified evidence or arguments also depends upon a balancing of how necessary the evidence is to a party's case and how imperative it is that the evidence remain secret.[45]

---

40. *El-Masri*, 479 F.3d at 304–06; *Sterling*, 416 F.3d at 343; *McDonnell Douglas Corp.*, 323 F.3d at 1021; *Kasza*, 133 F.3d at 1166; Black v. United States, 62 F.3d 1115, 1119 (8th Cir. 1995); *Zuckerbraun*, 935 F.2d at 546–47; *Fitzgerald*, 776 F.2d at 1243; *Halkin*, 690 F.2d at 990, 992–94.

41. *El-Masri*, 479 F.3d at 304, 306–13; *Kasza*, 133 F.3d at 1166; *Bareford*, 973 F.2d at 1141–44; *Halkin*, 690 F.2d at 990, 997–99; *Fitzgerald*, 776 F.2d at 1243; *Halpern*, 258 F.2d at 43–44.

42. United States v. Reynolds, 345 U.S. 1, 10 (1952).

43. Al-Haramain Islamic Found. v. Bush, 507 F.3d 1190, 1194 n.2 (9th Cir. 2007).

44. *Sterling*, 416 F.3d at 343–45; *Halkin*, 690 F.2d at 992–94.

45. *Sterling*, 416 F.3d at 343; Ellsberg v. Mitchell, 709 F.2d 51, 58–59 (D.C. Cir. 1983).

E. Disposition of the Case

Even tort cases have been dismissed because they could not be litigated without compromising state secrets.[46] If a plaintiff was denied access to state secrets essential to the plaintiff's claim, then the claim has been dismissed.[47] If a defendant was denied access to, or prevented from entering into evidence, state secrets that were essential to a defense, then also the claim has been dismissed.[48] Unavailability of material evidence, however, does not necessarily result in dismissal; sometimes the case is simply litigated without the unavailable evidence.[49]

If both the plaintiff and the defendant have access to state-secrets evidence, the court may be able to use various protective procedures to litigate the case without exposing state se-

---

46. *Sterling*, 416 F.3d at 345–48; *McDonnell Douglas Corp.*, 323 F.3d at 1021; *Kasza*, 133 F.3d at 166; *Fitzgerald*, 776 F.2d at 1243.

47. *McDonnell Douglas Corp.*, 323 F.3d at 1024; Monarch Assurance P.L.C. v. United States, 244 F.3d 1356, 1361 (Fed. Cir. 2001); *Kasza*, 133 F.3d at 166; Black v. United States, 62 F.3d 1115, 1119 (8th Cir. 1995); *Bareford*, 973 F.2d at 1142; *Zuckerbraun*, 935 F.2d at 547–48.

48. *In re* Sealed Case, 494 F.3d 139, 149 (D.C. Cir. 2007); *Sterling*, 416 F.3d at 344; Tenenbaum v. Simonini, 372 F.3d 776, 777 (6th Cir. 2004); *Kasza*, 133 F.3d at 166; Molerio v. FBI, 749 F.2d 815, 825 (D.C. Cir. 1984).

49. *In re Sealed Case*, 494 F.3d at 148 ("even after evidence relating to covert operatives, organizational structure and functions, and intelligence-gathering sources, methods, and capabilities is stricken from the proceedings under the state secrets privilege, [the plaintiff] has alleged sufficient facts to survive a motion to dismiss"); *Kasza*, 133 F.3d at 166; *In re* United States, 872 F.2d 472, 480 (D.C. Cir. 1989) ("We share the district court's confidence that it can police the litigation so as not to compromise national security."); Farnsworth Cannon, Inc. v. Grimes, 635 F.2d 268, 270–71 (4th Cir. 1980) ("When the government is not a party and successfully resists disclosure sought by a party, the result is simply that the evidence is unavailable, as though a witness had died, and the case will proceed accordingly, with no consequences save those resulting from the loss of the evidence.") (quoting McCormick's Handbook of the Law of Evidence § 109, at 233 (1972)).

crets to the public.[50] The case may also proceed if evidence is available that suitably substitutes for state-secrets evidence.[51]

III. The Classified Information Procedures Act

The Classified Information Procedures Act (CIPA) was enacted on October 15, 1980, and it is codified as the third appendix to Title 18 of the U.S. Code, the title concerning crimes and criminal procedures.[52]

CIPA, by its terms, covers only criminal cases; in civil cases, courts and the government follow procedures similar to those provided by CIPA.[53]

If either the government or the defendant believes that classified information will come into play in a criminal case, then that party must bring the matter to the court's attention, and the court must establish and implement procedures to keep classified information secret.[54]

---

50. Loral Corp. v. McDonnell Douglas Corp., 558 F.2d 1130, 1132 (2d Cir. 1977) ("[A] large amount of material properly classified confidential and secret must be submitted to the trier of fact in the case. We are persuaded that this circumstance is enough to make it inappropriate for jury trial."); Halpern v. United States, 258 F.2d 36, 43 (2d Cir. 1958) ("Under the circumstances of this case, we are not convinced that a trial in camera is either undesirable or unfeasible.").

51. United States v. Reynolds, 345 U.S. 1, 11 (1952) ("Here, necessity was greatly minimized by an available alternative, which might have given respondents the evidence to make out their case without forcing a showdown on the claim of privilege.").

52. The text of CIPA is reproduced in Appendix A.

53. 28 C.F.R. § 17.17(c) (2011).

54. United States v. Mejia, 448 F.3d 436, 455 (D.C. Cir. 2006) ("CIPA is a procedural statute that does not itself create a privilege against discovery of classified information."); United States v. O'Hara, 301 F.3d 563, 568 (7th Cir. 2002) ("CIPA's fundamental purpose [is] protecting and restricting the discovery of classified information in a way that does not impair the defendant's right to a fair trial."); United States v. Klimavicius-Viloria, 144 F.3d 1249, 1261 (9th Cir. 1998) ("Congress intended CIPA to clarify the court's power to restrict discovery of classified information."); United States v. Anderson, 872 F.2d 1508, 1514 (11th Cir. 1989) ("CIPA was enacted by Congress in an effort to combat the growing problem of greymail, a practice whereby a criminal defendant threatens to reveal classified information during the course of his trial in the hope of forcing the government to drop the criminal charge against him.").

IV. Bringing Classified Information to the Court's Attention

The court should receive prompt notice if classified information will be at play in a prosecution, and the court should promptly establish procedures to protect the information:

> At any time after the filing of the indictment or information, any party may move for a pretrial conference to consider matters relating to classified information that may arise in connection with the prosecution. Following such motion, or on its own motion, the court shall promptly hold a pretrial conference . . . .[55]

A. Classified Information Held by the Government

The government may bring concerns about classified information to the court's attention ex parte: "The court may permit the United States to make a request for [authorization to withhold classified information from the defendant] in the form of a written statement to be inspected by the court alone."[56]

If the court is to implement procedures to protect classified information, the government should provide the defendant with notice that classified information is at issue.[57]

> Before any [CIPA hearing], the United States shall provide the defendant with notice of the classified information that is at issue. Such notice shall identify the specific classified information at issue whenever that information previously has been made available to the defendant by the United States. When the United States has not previously made the information available to the defendant in connection with the case, the information may be described by generic category, in such form as the court may approve, rather than by identification of the specific information of concern to the United States.[58]

A court of appeals held that it was improper for a government agency to initiate secret proceedings, without the knowledge of either the defense or the prosecution, to determine

---

55. 18 U.S.C. app. 3 § 2 (2011).
56. *Id.* § 4; *see* United States v. Campa, 529 F.3d 980, 994–96 (11th Cir. 2008).
57. United States v. Baptista-Rodriguez, 17 F.3d 1354, 1363 (11th Cir. 1994).
58. 18 U.S.C. app. 3 § 6(b)(1) (2011).

whether certain classified information had to be disclosed to the defendant.[59]

B. Classified Information Held by a Defendant

If a criminal defendant contemplates use of classified information, the defendant must notify both the court and the government of its intentions.

> If a defendant reasonably expects to disclose or to cause the disclosure of classified information in any manner in connection with any trial or pretrial proceeding involving the criminal prosecution of such defendant, the defendant shall, within the time specified by the court or, where no time is specified, within thirty days prior to trial, notify the attorney for the United States and the court in writing. Such notice shall include a brief description of the classified information. Whenever a defendant learns of additional classified information he reasonably expects to disclose at any such proceeding, he shall notify the attorney for the United States and the court in writing as soon as possible thereafter and shall include a brief description of the classified information.[60]

A court of appeals held that "a brief description of the classified information," as prescribed in the text of the statute, is sufficient, overruling a trial court holding that the defendant's notice must include justifications of relevance.[61] But the notice must contain sufficient detail so that the government can determine how presentation of the evidence might damage national security.[62]

Evidence preclusion is the statutory remedy for failure to comply with the notice requirement.[63]

---

59. *Mejia*, 448 F.3d at 453–54 (concerning a district court finding in a drug-crime prosecution that classified evidence presented ex parte and in camera by the Drug Intelligence Unit of the Justice Department's Narcotic and Dangerous Drug Section would not be helpful to the defense).

60. 18 U.S.C. app. 3 § 5(a) (2011); *see* United States v. Rosen, 557 F.3d 192, 195 (4th Cir. 2009); United States v. Hashmi, 621 F. Supp. 2d 76, 81–82 (S.D.N.Y. 2008).

61. United States v. Miller, 874 F.2d 1255, 1276 (9th Cir. 1989).

62. United States v. Collins, 720 F.2d 1195, 1200 (11th Cir. 1983).

63. 18 U.S.C. app. 3 § 5(b) (2011); United States v. Badia, 827 F.2d 1458, 1464–66 (11th Cir. 1987).

V. Protective Procedures

A. CIPA Hearing

CIPA provides for a hearing to determine how classified evidence will be handled at trial. Although both parties may be present, the hearing may be conducted in camera if the government certifies that an in camera hearing is necessary to protect classified information.

> Within the time specified by the court for the filing of a motion under this section, the United States may request the court to conduct a hearing to make all determinations concerning the use, relevance, or admissibility of classified information that would otherwise be made during the trial or pretrial proceeding. Upon such a request, the court shall conduct such a hearing. Any hearing held pursuant to this subsection (or any portion of such hearing specified in the request of the Attorney General) shall be held in camera if the Attorney General certifies to the court in such petition that a public proceeding may result in the disclosure of classified information.[64]

The record of a hearing concerning classified information should be preserved for use in an appeal, but should be sealed to prevent unauthorized disclosure of the classified information.

> If at the close of an in camera hearing under this Act (or any portion of a hearing under this Act that is held in camera) the court determines that the classified information at issue may not be disclosed or elicited at the trial or pretrial proceeding, the record of such in camera hearing shall be sealed and preserved by the court for use in the event of an appeal. The defendant may seek reconsideration of the court's determination prior to or during trial.[65]

---

64. 18 U.S.C. app. 3 § 6(a) (2011); *see id.* § 6(c)(1) ("The court shall hold a hearing on any motion under this section. Any such hearing shall be held in camera at the request of the Attorney General."); *see also Rosen*, 557 F.3d at 195.
    65. *Id.* § 6(d).

Courts have also held ex parte CIPA hearings on the discoverability of classified evidence and on unclassified substitutions for classified evidence.[66]

B. Protective Orders

A key tool in protecting classified information is the protective order. "Upon motion of the United States, the court shall issue an order to protect against the disclosure of any classified information disclosed by the United States to any defendant in any criminal case in a district court of the United States."[67]

Courts have sometimes issued protective orders that forbid defense attorneys with security clearances from sharing classified discovery with their clients.[68]

C. Classification Designations

In the prosecution of Admiral John Poindexter for obstruction of Congress in the Iran–Contra scandal, the government produced in discovery hundreds of thousands of pages of documents, many of which were classified.[69] But the practices of the agencies who supplied the documents did not always result in the documents being marked to reflect their level of classification or precisely what parts of the documents were classified.[70] On the one hand, a full classification review of all of the documents would have been too burdensome for the government; but on the other hand, the defendant needed to know the classification status of documents he wanted to use for trial.[71] The parties negotiated a procedure, which was approved by the court, in which the defendant would identify documents he wanted to share with witnesses or use for trial, and an interagency group of government security officers would perform a full classifica-

---

66. United States v. Amawi, 695 F.3d 457, 472–73 (6th Cir. 2012); United States v. Aref, 533 F.3d 72, 81 (2d Cir. 2008); United States v. Campa, 529 F.3d 980, 994–95 (11th Cir. 2008); United States v. Klimavicius-Viloria, 144 F.3d 1249, 1261 (9th Cir. 1998).

67. *Id.* § 3; *see* Reagan, *supra* note 10, at 15.

68. *E.g.*, United States v. Moussaoui, 591 F.3d 263, 283 (4th Cir. 2010); *In re* Terrorist Bombings of U.S. Embassies in E. Africa, 552 F.3d 93, 115–30 (2d Cir. 2008).

69. United States v. Poindexter, 727 F. Supp. 1470, 1472, 1486 (D.D.C. 1989).

70. *Id.* at 1486 & n.33.

71. *Id.* at 1486.

tion review on those documents, but the group would not disclose to the attorneys representing the government which documents were reviewed.[72]

D. Withholding Discovery

Classified information may be withheld from the defendant.[73] The Act provides for three ways of withholding discovery: (1) deletion, (2) summarization, and (3) admission.

> The court, upon a sufficient showing, may authorize the United States to delete specified items of classified information, from documents to be made available to the defendant through discovery under the Federal Rules of Criminal Procedure, to substitute a summary of the information for such classified documents, or to substitute a statement admitting relevant facts that the classified information would tend to prove.[74]

The government must, however, provide the defendant with such information as is relevant and helpful to the defense.[75]

---

72. *Id.*

73. United States v. El-Mezain, 664 F.3d 467, 519–20 (5th Cir. 2011) ("CIPA is procedural and neither creates nor limits a defendant's right of discovery."); United States v. Hanna, 661 F.3d 271, 295 (6th Cir. 2011) ("CIPA does not itself create a government privilege against the disclosure of information; it presupposes one"); United States v. Aref, 533 F.3d 72, 78 (2d Cir. 2008) ("It is important to understand that CIPA section 4 *presupposed* a governmental privilege against disclosing classified information. It does not itself *create* a privilege.").

74. 18 U.S.C. app. 3 § 4 (2011); *see* United States v. Passaro, 577 F.3d 207, 220–21 (4th Cir. 2009) (approving the withholding in discovery of classified information pertaining to an authorization defense because the defendant offered no evidence of authorization); *In re* Terrorist Bombings of U.S. Embassies in E. Africa, 552 F.3d 93, 118–20 (2d Cir. 2008) (approving stipulations as substitutes for classified discovery); United States v. Ressam, 221 F. Supp. 2d 1252, 1256 (W.D. Wash. 2002) (in a prosecution for conspiracy to bomb the Los Angeles International Airport in December 1999, reviewing classified intelligence information potentially discoverable by the defendant and, after determining what was discoverable, authorizing the government to provide the defendant with unclassified summaries).

75. *Hanna*, 661 F.3d at 295 ("a district court withholding evidence under CIPA must first determine whether the material in dispute is discoverable, then whether the material is privileged, but then determine if the information is at least helpful to the defense" (internal quotation marks omitted)); United States v. Klimavicius-Viloria, 144 F.3d 1249, 1261 (9th Cir. 1998) ("In order to determine whether the government must disclose classified information, the court must

E. Ex Parte Presentation

To resolve discovery issues and pretrial motions, the government can present to the court in ex parte proceedings classified evidence to which neither the defendant nor defense counsel has access.[76] The court should make as much of a record of these proceedings as is consistent with protection of sensitive information.[77]

During the discovery phase of an obstruction-of-justice prosecution of Vice President Dick Cheney's chief of staff, the court permitted the government to submit ex parte potentially discoverable classified material for the court's review so long as the government explained why the material was classified and why defense counsel with security clearances could not see it.[78] The court also allowed defense counsel to submit ex parte to the court their defense needs so that the court could better evaluate whether the government's classified submissions were discoverable.[79]

In a prosecution for helping to fund Hamas, the defendant sought to suppress confession statements that he claimed were obtained with torture by Israeli secret police officers.[80] The governments of the United States and Israel waived the classification designation regarding all evidence presented at the suppression hearing, except for a small amount of evidence that concerned the credibility of the Israeli witnesses but not the defendant's treatment or guilt.[81] The court heard this evidence in

determine whether the information is 'relevant and helpful to the defense of an accused.'"); United States v. Rezaq, 134 F.3d 1121, 1142 (D.C. Cir. 1998) ("[I]f some portion or aspect of a document is classified, a defendant is entitled to receive it only if it may be helpful to his defense. A court applying this rule should, of course, err on the side of protecting the interests of the defendant."); United States v. Hanjuan Jin, 791 F. Supp. 2d 612, 620 (N.D. Ill. 2011) ("The Court will . . . give [the defendant] the benefit of the doubt in its analysis.").

76. *Hanna*, 661 F.3d at 294–95; United States v. Abu-Jihaad, 630 F.3d 102, 142–43 (2d Cir. 2010); *Klimavicius-Viloria*, 144 F.3d at 1261; United States v. Pringle, 751 F.2d 419, 427 (1st Cir. 1984).

77. United States v. Mejia, 448 F.3d 436, 453–54 (D.C. Cir. 2006).

78. United States v. Libby, 429 F. Supp. 2d 18, 25, 27 (D.D.C. 2006).

79. *Id.* at 26–27; *see also* United States v. North, 708 F. Supp. 389, 391 (D.D.C. 1988) (noting that the court obtained ex parte information about the intended defense before ordering extensive discovery on the government).

80. United States v. Marzook, 435 F. Supp. 2d 708 (N.D. Ill. 2006).

81. *Id.* at 745–47.

camera and ex parte.[82] Because the defense did not have access to this evidence, the court drew "adverse inferences" against the government, which the court explained were like a thumb on the scale in favor of the defendant—not drawing any inferences from the evidence in the government's favor.[83]

Appellate reviews of district court discovery rulings are sensitive to special considerations required by CIPA:

> When reviewing a district court's decision to withhold information under CIPA, this court is placed in a somewhat unfamiliar posture. Rather than neutrally deciding disputes with an open record based on the adversarial process, we must place ourselves in the shoes of defense counsel, the very ones that cannot see the classified record, and act with a view to their interests. Acting as if we were in essence standby counsel for the defendants, we must determine what may be "relevant and helpful" to them.[84]

F. Limited Presentation at Trial

The court may authorize the presentation of classified information at trial by summary or authorize admissions that would render the presentation of classified information unnecessary.[85] But the defendant must retain "substantially the same ability to make his defense as would disclosure of the specific classified information."[86]

> If the evidence would be admissible at trial, the burden shifts to the government to offer in lieu of the classified evidence either a statement admitting relevant facts that the classified information would tend to prove or a summary of the specific classified information. . . .
> . . . [But] the district court may not take into account the fact that evidence is classified when determining its use, relevance, or admissibility.[87]

In an espionage prosecution, the district court ruled that "although some of the government's proposed redactions were

82. *Id.* at 746.
83. *Id.* at 750.
84. United States v. Amawi, 695 F.3d 457, 471 (6th Cir. 2012).
85. 18 U.S.C. app. 3 § 6(c)(1) (2011).
86. *Id.*
87. United States v. Baptista-Rodriguez, 17 F.3d 1354, 1363–64 (11th Cir. 1994) (quotation marks omitted).

acceptable, other such redactions would not afford the defendants the same opportunity to defend themselves as would the admission of the unredacted documents containing classified information."[88] The district court ordered alternative substitutions over the government's objection.[89]

Some courts have held that normal evidentiary principles govern the admissibility of classified evidence.[90] For example, a district court ruled that classified evidence was admissible as part of a hijacking defendant's argument that the hijacking was a CIA operation.[91] Other courts require a balancing of the public interest in protecting secrets against the right to a defense.[92]

A court of appeals affirmed the trial court's allowing Israeli security officers to testify under the pseudonyms of Avi and Major Lior, without disclosing their true identities to the defense, in a prosecution for providing support to a charitable organization that helped to fund terrorism.[93] The court found "a serious and clear need to protect [their true identities] because of concerns for their safety."[94] The court also found that the defense was provided with substantial information about the witnesses that could be used for cross-examination, and because their identities were secret knowing their true identities may not have been very helpful in obtaining additional information about them.[95]

> The Government disclosed to the defense over twenty volumes of material that Avi used to formulate his expert opinion about Hamas financing. Moreover, the Government agreed in pretrial filings that the defense would be permitted to ask Avi about his background, his training and experience with the ISA, his legal education, and his potential bias in favor of Israelis in the West Bank. The defense was therefore well-

---

88. United States v. Rosen, 557 F.3d 192, 196 (4th Cir. 2009).

89. *Id.*; *see id.* at 200 (finding no abuse of discretion).

90. United States v. Anderson, 872 F.2d 1508, 1514 (11th Cir. 1989); United States v. Wilson, 750 F.2d 7, 9 (2d Cir. 1984).

91. United States v. Lopez-Lima, 738 F. Supp. 1404 (S.D. Fla. 1990).

92. United States v. Smith, 780 F.2d 1102, 1105 (4th Cir. 1985).

93. United States v. El-Mezain, 664 F.3d 467, 490–94 (5th Cir. 2011), *cert. denied*, 568 U.S. ___, 133 S. Ct. 525 (2012), *and cert. denied*, 568 U.S. ___, 133 S. Ct. 525 (2012).

94. *Id.* at 492.

95. *Id.* at 492–93.

armed with information upon which to confront and cross-examine both Avi and Major Lior, and a review of the trial record in fact shows that the defense was able to conduct effective cross-examination.[96]

Classified information may be presented to a jury without requiring security clearances for the jurors, but jurors may be cautioned not to disclose the classified information to others.[97]

When a defendant sought to prove that his confession was obtained with torture by Israeli secret police officers, the court permitted the government to make several admissions to obviate presentation of classified evidence.[98] For example, the government admitted that Israeli secret police officers were authorized to use hoods, handcuffs, and shackles during interrogations.[99] The defendant was able to question the police officers at trial about their treatment of him and "pursue extensive cross examination except in the limited areas that would elicit classified information."[100]

Courts have sometimes permitted narrowly tailored procedures that present classified evidence to the judge, the parties, and the jury, but not to the public.[101] A court of appeals held that it was improper for the district court to exclude the defendant himself, in a criminal trial, from a small amount of classified information presented to the jury.[102]

In a trial for conspiracy to communicate national defense information to unauthorized persons, the government sought to use a "silent witness" procedure extensively.[103] Using this procedure, the court, the witness, the parties, and the jury would have access to classified documents, but the public would not. Testimony concerning classified information would be in code, such as by referring to persons as X, Y, and Z, and by referring

---

96. *Id.* at 492.
97. Courts' Security Procedures, *supra* note 9, ¶ 6.
98. United States v. Salah, 462 F. Supp. 2d 915, 917–18, 925 (N.D. Ill. 2006).
99. *Id.* at 917.
100. *Id.* at 923, 925.
101. *E.g.*, United States v. Pelton, 696 F. Supp. 156 (D. Md. 1986) (allowing the playing of audiotapes containing "secret" information through headphones).
102. United States v. Abu Ali, 528 F.3d 210, 254–55 (4th Cir. 2008).
103. United States v. Rosen, 487 F. Supp. 2d 703, 705–09 (E.D. Va. 2007); *see also* United States v. Zettl, 835 F.2d 1059, 1063 (4th Cir. 1987) (describing the silent witness rule).

to countries as A, B, and C. The trial judge ruled that extensive use of this procedure would impair the defendant's statutory right to make his defense and his constitutional right to a public trial.[104]

> [I]t is appropriate to approve use of the [silent witness rule] only when the government establishes (i) an overriding reason for closing the trial, (ii) that the closure is no broader than necessary to protect that interest, (iii) that no reasonable alternatives exist to closure, and (iv) that the use of the [silent witness rule] provides defendants with substantially the same ability to make their defense as full public disclosure of the evidence, presented without the use of codes.[105]

G. Declassification

Once the court determines what classified evidence must be admitted to ensure the defendant a fair trial, the government may decide to declassify the information.[106]

H. Jury Instructions

It may be helpful to instruct the jury on why trial proceedings appear to be skirting relevant information. One judge developed the following instruction:

> This case involves certain classified information. Classified information is information or material that has been determined by the United States Government pursuant to an Executive order, statute, or regulation, to require protection against unauthorized disclosure. In lieu of disclosing specific classified information, I anticipate that you will hear certain substitutions for the classified information during this trial. These substitutions are admissions of relevant facts by the United States for purposes of this trial. The witnesses in this case as well as attorneys are prohibited from disclosing clas-

---

104. *Rosen*, 487 F. Supp. 2d at 714, 720; *see Abu Ali*, 528 F.3d at 255 n.22 ("We are not called upon and express no opinion as to whether use of the 'silent witness' procedure would have been proper had defendant received the same document presented to the jury.").

105. United States v. Rosen, 520 F. Supp. 2d 786, 799 (E.D. Va. 2007); *see id.* at 796–97 (noting that the silent witness rule is a judicially created mechanism for handling classified information at trial separate from the provisions of the Classified Information Procedures Act).

106. United States v. O'Hara, 301 F.3d 563, 568 (7th Cir. 2002).

sified information and, in the case of the attorneys, are prohibited from asking questions to any witness which if answered would disclose classified information. Defendants may not cross examine a particular witness regarding the underlying classified matters set forth in these admissions. You must decide what weight, if any, to give to these admissions.[107]

I. Dismissal

If the government's secrets cannot be protected adequately while affording the defendant a fair trial, then ordinarily the indictment is dismissed.[108]

VI. Flexibility

At the conclusion of the trial of Colonel Oliver North for his involvement in the Iran–Contra scandal, Judge Gerhard Gesell observed that the court and the attorneys served the purposes of CIPA, although they did not always conform to CIPA precisely.

> CIPA was ill-suited to a case of this type and amendments are needed to recognize practical difficulties. For some instances, the Court followed procedures which were not in strict accord with the statutory framework to expedite resolution of unusual problems that arose. Fortunately, CIPA is a procedural statute, and the legislative history of it shows that Congress expected trial judges to fashion creative solutions in the interests of justice for classified information problems. The Executive cooperated with the Court by liberally waiving classification objections when to do otherwise might have halted the proceeding and interfered with a fair trial.[109]

VII. Interlocutory Appeal

The government has a statutory right to an expedited interlocutory appeal of an order "authorizing the disclosure of classified information, imposing sanctions for nondisclosure of classified

107. United States v. Salah, 462 F. Supp. 2d 915, 924 (N.D. Ill. 2006).
108. United States v. Moussaoui, 382 F.3d 453, 466 n.18, 474–76 (4th Cir. 2004).
109. United States v. North, 713 F. Supp. 1452, 1452–53 (D.D.C. 1989).

information, or refusing a protective order sought by the United States to prevent the disclosure of classified information."[110]

VIII. Classified Information Security Officers

The Department of Justice employs security specialists whose job it is to assist the courts in protecting the secrecy of classified information.

There are nine security specialists who are employed by the Department of Justice's Security and Emergency Planning Staff (SEPS) and detailed to the courts as classified information security officers. They, plus an associate director of SEPS, two personnel security specialists, and two security assistants, constitute the Litigation Security Group, which is approximately one eighth of SEPS's personnel. The director of SEPS reports to the deputy assistant attorney general for Human Resources and Administration, a unit of the Department of Justice's Justice Management Division, which is headed by an assistant attorney general. This assistant attorney general is designated by regulation as the Justice Department's manager of information classification and access to classified information.[111]

The classified information security officers are not lawyers, and they are organizationally quite separate from the government's representatives in court. Their obligation is to help the court protect classified information, not to assist the government's representatives in court.[112] In fact, they often provide assistance to parties opposing the government.

Formally, in criminal cases, when the court needs assistance in protecting classified information, the director of SEPS submits to the presiding judge a nomination letter recommending a security specialist as the court's classified information security officer. This nomination letter complies with procedures estab-

---

110. 18 U.S.C. app. 3 § 7(a) (2011); *see* United States v. Rosen, 557 F.3d 192, 196–98 (4th Cir. 2009).
111. 28 C.F.R. § 17.11(a) (2011).
112. United States v. Yunis, 867 F.2d 617, 621 n.8 (D.C. Cir. 1989); United States v. Musa, 833 F. Supp. 752, 756 (E.D. Mo. 1993).

lished by the Chief Justice, as required by CIPA.[113] The director of SEPS customarily recommends one security specialist as the classified information security officer for the case and recommends several others as alternates.

The Litigation Security Group's personnel security specialists help court staff and defense attorneys obtain security clearances as necessary and appropriate.

IX. Sensitive Compartmented Information Facilities

The classified information security officer will assist the court in determining how to physically secure classified documents. Sometimes a safe in the judge's chambers is enough. Sometimes classified documents must be stored in a "Sensitive Compartmented Information Facility," or SCIF.

A SCIF (which usually is pronounced like "skiff") is a secure room—or building—that meets certain construction and access requirements. Courthouses where cases implicating classified information arise frequently—such as the Southern District of New York and the Eastern District of Virginia—have one or more SCIFs. Attorneys—and their clients if they have sufficient security clearances—may be required to review classified information within a SCIF.

Typically, separate safes within a SCIF are designated for separate cases. Judges, court staff, and attorneys are only granted access to material stored in a SCIF for which their access is necessary.

When a SCIF is required for a court to hear a case, the classified information security officer will either construct a SCIF for the court or arrange for the court to have access to an existing SCIF.[114] The classified information security officer works with judges, the clerk's office, and the marshals service to designate appropriate space for construction of a SCIF. Sometimes, savings can be achieved by designating a space that requires modest modifications. Also, if need for a SCIF is intermittent,

---

113. Courts' Security Procedures, *supra* note 9.
114. Construction expenses are borne by the executive branch. *Id.* ¶ 12.

sometimes space can be fitted for a SCIF, returned to regular service when the SCIF is not needed, and then fitted for a SCIF later if necessary.

X. Conclusion

The executive branch decides what information is classified as state secrets, and the judicial branch decides how to protect the rights of parties in civil and criminal cases while keeping government secrets. The Classified Information Procedures Act and classified information security officers help the courts meet their obligations to the parties and the government.

Appendix A:
Classified Information Procedures Act[115]

§ 1. Definitions

(a) "Classified information," as used in this Act, means any information or material that has been determined by the United States Government pursuant to an Executive order, statute, or regulation, to require protection against unauthorized disclosure for reasons of national security and any restricted data, as defined in paragraph r. of section 11 of the Atomic Energy Act of 1954 (42 U.S.C. 2014(y)).

(b) "National security," as used in this Act, means the national defense and foreign relations of the United States.

§ 2. Pretrial Conference

At any time after the filing of the indictment or information, any party may move for a pretrial conference to consider matters relating to classified information that may arise in connection with the prosecution. Following such motion, or on its own motion, the court shall promptly hold a pretrial conference to establish the timing of requests for discovery, the provision of notice required by section 5 of this Act, and the initiation of the procedure established by section 6 of this Act. In addition, at the pretrial conference the court may consider any matters which relate to classified information or which may promote a fair and expeditious trial. No admission made by the defendant or by any attorney for the defendant at such a conference may be used against the defendant unless the admission is in writing and is signed by the defendant and by the attorney for the defendant.

§ 3. Protective Orders

Upon motion of the United States, the court shall issue an order to protect against the disclosure of any classified information disclosed by the United States to any defendant in any criminal case in a district court of the United States.

---

115. 18 U.S.C. app. 3 (2011), enacted by Pub. L. 96-456, 94 Stat. 2025 (1980).

§ 4. Discovery of Classified Information by Defendants

The court, upon a sufficient showing, may authorize the United States to delete specified items of classified information from documents to be made available to the defendant through discovery under the Federal Rules of Criminal Procedure, to substitute a summary of the information for such classified documents, or to substitute a statement admitting relevant facts that the classified information would tend to prove. The court may permit the United States to make a request for such authorization in the form of a written statement to be inspected by the court alone. If the court enters an order granting relief following such an ex parte showing, the entire text of the statement of the United States shall be sealed and preserved in the records of the court to be made available to the appellate court in the event of an appeal.

§ 5. Notice of Defendant's Intention to Disclose Classified Information

(a) Notice by Defendant

If a defendant reasonably expects to disclose or to cause the disclosure of classified information in any manner in connection with any trial or pretrial proceeding involving the criminal prosecution of such defendant, the defendant shall, within the time specified by the court or, where no time is specified, within thirty days prior to trial, notify the attorney for the United States and the court in writing. Such notice shall include a brief description of the classified information. Whenever a defendant learns of additional classified information he reasonably expects to disclose at any such proceeding, he shall notify the attorney for the United States and the court in writing as soon as possible thereafter and shall include a brief description of the classified information. No defendant shall disclose any information known or believed to be classified in connection with a trial or pretrial proceeding until notice has been given under this subsection and until the United States has been afforded a reasonable opportunity to seek a determination pursuant to the procedure set forth in section 6 of this Act, and until the time for the United States to appeal such determination under section 7 has expired or any appeal under section 7 by the United States is decided.

(b) Failure to Comply

If the defendant fails to comply with the requirements of subsection (a) the court may preclude disclosure of any classified information not made the subject of notification and may prohibit the examination by the defendant of any witness with respect to any such information.

§ 6. Procedure for Cases Involving Classified Information

(a) Motion for Hearing

Within the time specified by the court for the filing of a motion under this section, the United States may request the court to conduct a hearing to make all determinations concerning the use, relevance, or admissibility of classified information that would otherwise be made during the trial or pretrial proceeding. Upon such a request, the court shall conduct such a hearing. Any hearing held pursuant to this subsection (or any portion of such hearing specified in the request of the Attorney General) shall be held in camera if the Attorney General certifies to the court in such petition that a public proceeding may result in the disclosure of classified information. As to each item of classified information, the court shall set forth in writing the basis for its determination. Where the United States' motion under this subsection is filed prior to the trial or pretrial proceeding, the court shall rule prior to the commencement of the relevant proceeding.

(b) Notice

(1) Before any hearing is conducted pursuant to a request by the United States under subsection (a), the United States shall provide the defendant with notice of the classified information that is at issue. Such notice shall identify the specific classified information at issue whenever that information previously has been made available to the defendant by the United States. When the United States has not previously made the information available to the defendant in connection with the case, the information may be described by generic category, in

such forms as the court may approve, rather than by identification of the specific information of concern to the United States.

(2) Whenever the United States requests a hearing under subsection (a), the court, upon request of the defendant, may order the United States to provide the defendant, prior to trial, such details as to the portion of the indictment or information at issue in the hearing as are needed to give the defendant fair notice to prepare for the hearing.

(c) Alternative Procedure for Disclosure of Classified Information

(1) Upon any determination by the court authorizing the disclosure of specific classified information under the procedures established by this section, the United States may move that, in lieu of the disclosure of such specific classified information, the court order—

(A) the substitution for such classified information of a statement admitting relevant facts that the specific classified information would tend to prove; or

(B) the substitution for such classified information of a summary of the specific classified information.

The court shall grant such a motion of the United States if it finds that the statement or summary will provide the defendant with substantially the same ability to make his defense as would disclosure of the specific classified information. The court shall hold a hearing on any motion under this section. Any such hearing shall be held in camera at the request of the Attorney General.

(2) The United States may, in connection with a motion under paragraph (1), submit to the court an affidavit of the Attorney General certifying that disclosure of classified information would cause identifiable damage to the national security of the United States and explaining the basis for the classification of such information. If so requested by the United States, the court shall examine such affidavit in camera and ex parte.

(d) Sealing of Records of In Camera Hearings

If at the close of an in camera hearing under this Act (or any portion of a hearing under this Act that is held in camera) the court determines that the classified information at issue may not be disclosed or elicited at the trial or pretrial proceeding, the record of such in camera hearing shall be sealed and preserved by the court for use in the event of an appeal. The defendant may seek reconsideration of the court's determination prior to or during trial.

(e) Prohibition on Disclosure of Classified Information by Defendant, Relief for Defendant When United States Opposes Disclosure

(1) Whenever the court denies a motion by the United States that it issue an order under subsection (c) and the United States files with the court an affidavit of the Attorney General objecting to disclosure of the classified information at issue, the court shall order that the defendant not disclose or cause the disclosure of such information.

(2) Whenever a defendant is prevented by an order under paragraph (1) from disclosing or causing the disclosure of classified information, the court shall dismiss the indictment or information; except that, when the court determines that the interests of justice would not be served by dismissal of the indictment or information, the court shall order such other action, in lieu of dismissing the indictment or information, as the court determines is appropriate. Such action may include, but need not be limited to—

(A) dismissing specified counts of the indictment or information;

(B) finding against the United States on any issue as to which the excluded classified information relates; or

(C) striking or precluding all or part of the testimony of a witness.

An order under this paragraph shall not take effect until the court has afforded the United States an opportunity to appeal such order under section 7, and thereafter to withdraw its objection to the disclosure of the classified information at issue.

(f) Reciprocity

Whenever the court determines pursuant to subsection (a) that classified information may be disclosed in connection with a trial or pretrial proceeding, the court shall, unless the interests of fairness do not so require, order the United States to provide the defendant with the information it expects to use to rebut the classified information. The court may place the United States under a continuing duty to disclose such rebuttal information. If the United States fails to comply with its obligation under this subsection, the court may exclude any evidence not made the subject of a required disclosure and may prohibit the examination by the United States of any witness with respect to such information.

§ 7. Interlocutory Appeal

(a) An interlocutory appeal by the United States taken before or after the defendant has been placed in jeopardy shall lie to a court of appeals from a decision or order of a district court in a criminal case authorizing the disclosure of classified information, imposing sanctions for nondisclosure of classified information, or refusing a protective order sought by the United States to prevent the disclosure of classified information.

(b) An appeal taken pursuant to this section either before or during trial shall be expedited by the court of appeals. Prior to trial, an appeal shall be taken within fourteen days[116] after the decision or order appealed from and the trial shall not commence until the appeal is resolved. If an appeal is taken during trial, the trial court shall adjourn the trial until the appeal is resolved and the court of appeals (1) shall hear argument on such appeal within four days of the adjournment of the trial, excluding intermediate weekends and holidays,[117] (2) may dispense with written briefs other than the supporting materials previously submitted to the trial court, (3) shall render its decision within four days of argument on appeal, excluding intermediate weekends and holidays, and (4) may dispense with the issuance of a written opinion in rendering its decision. Such appeal and decision shall not affect the right of the defendant, in a subsequent appeal from a judgment of conviction, to claim as error reversal by the trial court on remand of a ruling appealed from during trial.

---

116. Fourteen days substituted for ten days by the Statutory Time-Periods Technical Amendments Act of 2009, Pub. L. 111-16, 123 Stat. 1607, 1608.

117. The phrase "excluding weekends and holidays," which appears twice in this paragraph, was added by the Statutory Time-Periods Technical Amendments Act of 2009, *id.*

§ 8. Introduction of Classified Information

(a) Classification Status
Writings, recordings, and photographs containing classified information may be admitted into evidence without change in their classification status.

(b) Precautions by Court
The court, in order to prevent unnecessary disclosure of classified information involved in any criminal proceeding, may order admission into evidence of only part of a writing, recording, or photograph, or may order admission into evidence of the whole writing, recording, or photograph with excision of some or all of the classified information contained therein, unless the whole ought in fairness be considered.

(c) Taking of Testimony
During the examination of a witness in any criminal proceeding, the United States may object to any question or line of inquiry that may require the witness to disclose classified information not previously found to be admissible. Following such an objection, the court shall take such suitable action to determine whether the response is admissible as will safeguard against the compromise of any classified information. Such action may include requiring the United States to provide the court with a proffer of the witness' response to the question or line of inquiry and requiring the defendant to provide the court with a proffer of the nature of the information he seeks to elicit.

§ 9. Security Procedures

(a) Within one hundred and twenty days of the date of the enactment of this Act, the Chief Justice of the United States, in consultation with the Attorney General, the Director of National Intelligence,[118] and the Secretary of Defense, shall prescribe rules[119] establishing procedures for the protection against unauthorized disclosure of any classified information in the cus-

118. Director of National Intelligence substituted for Director of Central Intelligence by the Intelligence Reform and Terrorism Prevention Act of 2004, Pub. L. 108-458, 118 Stat. 3638, 3691.
119. *See* Appendix B.

tody of the United States district courts, courts of appeal, or Supreme Court. Such rules, and any changes in such rules, shall be submitted to the appropriate committees of Congress and shall become effective forty-five days after such submission.

(b) Until such time as rules under subsection (a) first become effective, the Federal courts shall in each case involving classified information adapt procedures to protect against the unauthorized disclosure of such information.

§ 9A. Coordination Requirements Relating to the Prosecution of Cases Involving Classified Information[120]

(a) Briefing Required

The Assistant Attorney General for the Criminal Division or the Assistant Attorney General for National Security, as appropriate,[121] and the appropriate United States attorney, or the designees of such officials, shall provide briefings to the senior agency official, or the designee of such official, with respect to any case involving classified information that originated in the agency of such senior agency official.

(b) Timing of Briefings

Briefings under subsection (a) with respect to a case shall occur—

(1) as soon as practicable after the Department of Justice and the United States attorney concerned determine that a prosecution or potential prosecution could result; and

(2) at such other times thereafter as are necessary to keep the senior agency official concerned fully and currently informed of the status of the prosecution.

(c) Senior Agency Official Defined

In this section, the term "senior agency official" has the meaning given that term in section 1.1 of Executive Order No. 12958.

---

120. This section was added by the Intelligence Authorization Act for Fiscal Year 2001, Pub. L. 106-567, 114 Stat. 2831, 2855–56 (2000).

121. The phrase "or the Assistant Attorney General for National Security, as appropriate" was added by the USA PATRIOT Improvement and Reauthorization Act of 2005, Pub. L. 109-177, 120 Stat. 192, 248.

§ 10. Identification of Information Related to the National Defense

In any prosecution in which the United States must establish that material relates to the national defense or constitutes classified information, the United States shall notify the defendant, within the time before trial specified by the court, of the portions of the material that it reasonably expects to rely upon to establish the national defense or classified information element of the offense.

§ 11. Amendments to the Act

Sections 1 through 10 of this Act may be amended as provided in section 2076, title 28, United States Code.

§ 12. Attorney General Guidelines

(a) Within one hundred and eighty days of enactment of this Act, the Attorney General shall issue guidelines specifying the factors to be used by the Department of Justice in rendering a decision whether to prosecute a violation of Federal law in which, in the judgment of the Attorney General, there is a possibility that classified information will be revealed. Such guidelines shall be transmitted to the appropriate committees of Congress.

(b) When the Department of Justice decides not to prosecute a violation of Federal law pursuant to subsection (a), an appropriate official of the Department of Justice shall prepare written findings detailing the reasons for the decision not to prosecute. The findings shall include—

(1) the intelligence information which the Department of Justice officials believe might be disclosed,

(2) the purpose for which the information might be disclosed,

(3) the probability that the information would be disclosed, and

(4) the possible consequences such disclosure would have on the national security.

§ 13. Reports to Congress

(a) Consistent with applicable authorities and duties, including those conferred by the Constitution upon the executive and legislative branches, the Attorney General shall report orally or in writing semiannually to the Permanent Select Committee on Intelligence of the United States House of Representatives, the Select Committee on Intelligence of the United States Senate, and the chairmen and ranking minority members of the Committees on the Judiciary of the Senate and House of Representatives on all cases where a decision not to prosecute a violation of Federal law pursuant to section 12(a) has been made.

(b)[122] In the case of the semiannual reports (whether oral or written) required to be submitted under subsection (a) to the Permanent Select Committee on Intelligence of the House of Representatives and the Select Committee on Intelligence of the Senate, the submittal dates for such reports shall be as provided in section 507 of the National Security Act of 1947.

(c) The Attorney General shall deliver to the appropriate committees of Congress a report concerning the operation and effectiveness of this Act and including suggested amendments to this Act. For the first three years this Act is in effect, there shall be a report each year. After three years, such reports shall be delivered as necessary.

§ 14. Functions of Attorney General May Be Exercised by Deputy Attorney General, the Associate Attorney General, or a Designated Assistant Attorney General

The functions and duties of the Attorney General under this Act may be exercised by the Deputy Attorney General, the Associate Attorney General,[123] or by an Assistant Attorney General designated by the Attorney General for such purpose and may not be delegated to any other official.

---

122. This subsection was added by the Intelligence Authorization Act for Fiscal Year 2003, Pub. L. 107-306, 116 Stat. 2383, 2423 (2002).

123. The Associate Attorney General was added to this list by the Anti-Drug Abuse Act of 1988, Pub. L. 100-690, 102 Stat. 4181, 4396.

§ 15. Effective Date

The provisions of this Act shall become effective upon the date of the enactment of this Act, but shall not apply to any prosecution in which an indictment or information was filed before such date.

§ 16. Short Title

That this Act may be cited as the "Classified Information Procedures Act."

Appendix B:
Security Procedures Established Pursuant to PL 96-456, 94 Stat. 2025, by the Chief Justice of the United States for the Protection of Classified Information[124]

1. Purpose. The purpose of these procedures, as revised, is to meet the requirements of Section 9(a) of the Classified Information Procedures Act of 1980, Pub. L. 96-456, 94 Stat. 2025, as amended ("the Act"), which in pertinent part provides that:

> ". . . [T]he Chief Justice of the United States, in consultation with the Attorney General, the Director of National Intelligence, and the Secretary of Defense, shall prescribe rules establishing procedures for the protection against unauthorized disclosure of any classified information in the custody of the United States district courts, courts of appeal, or Supreme Court. . . ."

These revised procedures apply in all criminal proceedings involving classified information, and appeals therefrom, before the United States district courts, the courts of appeal and the Supreme Court, and supersede the Security Procedures issued on February 12, 1981.

2. Classified Information Security Officer. In any proceeding in a criminal case or appeal therefrom in which classified information is within, or is reasonably expected to be within, the custody of the court, the court will designate a "classified information security officer." The Attorney General or the Department of Justice Security Officer will recommend to the court a person qualified to serve as a classified information security officer. This individual will be selected from the Litigation Security Group, Security and Emergency Planning Staff, Department of Justice, to be detailed to the court to serve in a neutral capacity. The court may designate, as required, one or more alternate classified information security officers who have been recommended in the manner specified above.

The classified information security officer must be an individual with demonstrated competence in security matters. Prior to designation, the Department of Justice Security Officer must

---

124. Effective Jan. 15, 2011, 18 U.S.C. app. 3 § 9 note (2013).

certify in writing that the classified information security officer is properly cleared, i.e., possesses the necessary clearance for the level and category of classified information involved.

The classified information security officer will be responsible to the court for the security of all classified information in the court's custody, including, but not limited to, any pleadings or other filings created in connection with the proceedings, and any form of information contained in any format, including testimony, notes, photographs, transcripts, documents, digital files, audio files or video files, stored on any type of equipment (*e.g.*, computers, electronic storage devices, etc.). In addition, any matters relating to personnel, information, or communications security will be the responsibility of the classified information security officer who will take measures reasonably necessary to fulfill these responsibilities. The classified information security officer must notify the court and the Department of Justice Security Officer of any actual, attempted, or potential violation of security procedures.

3. Secure Location. Any in camera proceeding—including, but not limited to, a pretrial conference, motion hearing, status hearing, suppression hearing, substitution hearing, or appellate proceeding—concerning the use, relevance, or admissibility of classified information must be held in a secure location recommended by the classified information security officer and approved by the court.

The secure location must be within the federal courthouse, unless it is determined that no available location in the courthouse meets, or can reasonably be adapted to meet, the security requirements of the Executive Branch applicable to the level and category of classified information involved. In the event that no suitable location exists within the courthouse, upon recommendation by the classified information security officer, the court will designate another United States Government facility located within the vicinity of the courthouse, as the secure location.

The classified information security officer must make necessary arrangements to ensure that the security requirements of the Executive Branch applicable to the level and category of classified information involved are met and must conduct or arrange for such inspection of the secure location as may be necessary. The classified information security officer must, in consultation with the United States Marshal, arrange for the installation of security devices and take such other measures as may be necessary to protect against any unauthorized access to or disclosure of classified information. All of the aforementioned activities must be conducted in a manner that does not interfere with the orderly proceedings of the court. Prior to any hearing or other proceeding, the classified information security officer must certify to the court that the location to be used is secure.

4. Personnel Security—Court Personnel. No person appointed by the court or designated for service therein will be given access to any classified information in the custody of the court, unless such person has received the appropriate security clearance and unless access to such information is necessary for the performance of an official function. A security clearance for justices and other Article III judges is not required.

The court shall timely notify the classified information security officer of the names of court personnel who may require access to classified information. The classified information security officer will then notify the Department of Justice Security Officer, who will promptly make arrangements to obtain any necessary security clearances. All security clearance requests will be reviewed and determinations will be made in accordance with the adjudication standards of the Executive Branch applicable to the level and category of classified information involved. The classified information security officer, on behalf of the Department of Justice Security Officer, will advise the court when the necessary security clearances have been obtained. When necessary, the court may request that security clearances for certain court personnel be expedited.

If security clearances cannot be obtained promptly, United States Government personnel possessing the appropriate security clearances may be temporarily assigned to assist the court. If a proceeding is required to be recorded and an official court reporter having the necessary security clearance is unavailable, the court may request the classified information security officer or the attorney for the government to have a cleared reporter designated to act as a reporter in the proceedings. The reporter so designated must take the oath of office as prescribed by 28 U.S.C. § 753(a).

Justices, judges and cleared court personnel may disclose classified information only to persons who possess both the appropriate security clearance and the requisite need to know the information in the performance of an official function. However, nothing contained in these procedures precludes a judge from performing his or her official duties, including giving appropriate instructions to a jury.

Any security concern regarding classified information and involving court personnel or persons acting for the court must be referred to the court and the Department of Justice Security Officer for appropriate action.

5. Persons Acting for the Defense. The government may obtain information by any lawful means concerning the trustworthiness of persons associated with the defense and may bring such information to the attention of the court for the court's consideration in framing an appropriate protective order pursuant to Section 3 of the Act.

6. Jury. Nothing contained in these procedures will be construed to require an investigation or security clearance of the members of a jury or to interfere with the functions of a jury, including access to classified information introduced as evidence in the trial of a case.

At any time during trial, the trial judge should consider, based on a party request or *sua sponte*, giving the jury a cautionary instruction regarding the release or disclosure of any classified information provided to the jury.

7. Custody and Storage of Classified Materials.

a. Materials Covered. These security procedures apply to any classified information, as the term is defined in Section 1(a) of the Act, that is in the custody of the court. This includes, but is not limited to any pleadings or other filings created in connection with the proceedings, and any form of information contained in any format, such as testimony, notes, photographs, transcripts, documents, digital files, audio files or video files, stored on any type of equipment (*e.g.*, computers, electronic storage devices, etc.).

b. Safekeeping. Classified information submitted to the court must be placed in the custody of the classified information security officer or appropriately cleared court personnel who will then be responsible for its safekeeping. When not in use, all classified materials must be stored in a safe that conforms to the General Services Administration standards for security containers. Classified information will be segregated from other information unrelated to the case at hand by securing it in a separate security container. If the court does not possess a storage container that meets the required standards, the necessary storage container or containers are to be supplied to the court on a temporary basis by the appropriate Executive Branch agency as determined by the Department of Justice Security Officer. Only the classified information security officer, alternate classified information security officer(s), and appropriately cleared court personnel will have access to the combination and the contents of the container.

For other than temporary storage (*e.g.*, a brief court recess), the classified information security officer must ensure that the storage area in which these containers will be located meets Executive Branch standards applicable to the level and category of classified information involved. The secure storage area may be located within either the federal courthouse or the facilities of another United States Government agency.

c. Transmittal of Classified Information. During the pendency of any hearing, trial or appeal, classified materials stored in the facilities of another United States Government agency must be transmitted to and from the court in the manner prescribed by the Executive Branch security regulations applicable to the level and category of classified information involved. A trust receipt must accompany all classified materials transmitted and must be signed by the recipient and returned to the classified information security officer.

8. Operating Routine.

a. Access to Court Records. Court personnel will have access to court records containing classified information only as authorized. Access to classified information by court personnel will be limited to the minimum number of cleared persons necessary for operational purposes. Access includes presence at any proceeding during which classified information may be disclosed. Arrangements for access to classified information in the custody of the court by court personnel and by persons acting for the defense must be approved in advance by the court, which may issue a protective order concerning such access.

b. Access to Other Discoverable Information. Except as otherwise authorized by a protective order, persons acting for the defense will not be given custody of classified information provided by the government. They may, at the discretion of the court, be afforded access to classified information provided by the government in secure locations that have been approved in accordance with § 3 of these procedures, but such classified information must remain in the control of the classified information security officer. The classified information security officer also will control access to classified information in the possession of the defense that is filed with the court or is reasonably expected to come within the custody of the court.

c. Telephone and Computer Security. Classified information must not be discussed, communicated, or processed using any non-secure communication device including standard commercial telephone instruments or office intercommunication systems, cellular devices, computers, and/or other electronic or internet-based communication services. Classified information may only be discussed, communicated and processed on devices cleared for the level of classification of the information to be disclosed or processed as approved by the Classified Information Security Officer.

d. Disposal of Classified Material. The classified information security officer is responsible for the secure disposal of all classified materials in the custody of the court which are not otherwise required to be retained.

9. Records Security.

a. Classification Markings. The classified information security officer, after consultation with the appropriate classification authority, is responsible for marking all court materials containing classified information with the appropriate level of classification, and for indicating thereon any special access controls that also appear on the face of the material from which the classified information was obtained or that are otherwise applicable.

Any and all materials potentially containing classified information filed by the defense must be filed under seal with the classified information security officer. The classified information security officer may permit counsel to file, on the public docket, non-substantive pleadings or documents (*e.g.*, motions for extension of time, scheduling matters, continuances, etc.) that do not contain information that is or may be classified. The classified information security officer must promptly coordinate with the appropriate classification authority to determine whether each filing contains classified information. If it is determined that the filed material does contain classified information, the classified information security officer must ensure that it is marked with the appropriate classification markings. If it is determined that the filed material does not contain classified information, it should be unsealed and placed in the public record. Upon the request of the government, the court may direct that any filed materials containing classified information must thereafter be maintained in accordance with § 7 of these procedures.

b. Accountability System. The classified information security officer is responsible for the establishment and maintenance of a control and accountability system for all classified information received by or transmitted from the court. Upon request, the classified information security officer will provide to the court an inventory of all classified information received by the court.

10. Transmittal of the Record on Appeal. The record on appeal, or any portion thereof, which contains classified information must be transmitted to the court of appeals or to the Supreme Court in the manner specified in § 7(c) of these procedures.

Any court records containing classified information must be maintained, through the pendency of any direct appeal, at a secure location that is reasonably accessible and approved by the classified information security officer, and must be stored in a proper security container.

11. Final Disposition. Within a reasonable time after all proceedings in the case have been concluded, including appeals, the court will release to the classified information security officer all materials containing classified information. The classified information security officer will then transmit them to the Department of Justice Security Officer to be maintained in accordance with approved storage procedures. The materials must be transmitted in the manner specified in § 7(c) of these procedures and must be accompanied by the appropriate accountability records required by § 9(b) of these procedures.

12. Expenses. All expenses of the United States Government that arise in connection with the implementation of these procedures, including any construction or equipment costs, will be borne by the Department of Justice and other appropriate Executive Branch agencies whose classified information is being protected.

13. Interpretation. Any question concerning the interpretation of any security requirement contained in these procedures will be resolved by the court in consultation with the Classified Information Security Officer who will consult with the Department of Justice Security Officer, if necessary.

14. Term. These revised procedures remain in effect until modified in writing by The Chief Justice after consultation with the Attorney General of the United States, the Director of National Intelligence, and the Secretary of Defense.

15. Effective Date. These revised procedures become effective forty-five days after the date of submission to the appropriate Congressional Committees, as required by the Act.

Issued this 1st day of December, 2010,[125] after taking into account the views of the Attorney General of the United States, the Director of National Intelligence, and the Secretary of Defense, as required by law.

---

125. "[These] rules, and any changes in [these] rules, shall be submitted to the appropriate committees of Congress and shall become effective forty-five days after such submission." 18 U.S.C. app. 3 § 9(a) (2011).